Praise F

"She was like blood. Me ana ner together had this chemis-try....Beyond the music she was a brilliant person...the most special person I ever met."
—Timbaland, Producer, Rapper

"She was like one of my daughters. She was one of the sweetest girls in the world."
—Quincy Jones, Producer, Arranger

Aaliyah was the first person to embrace Destiny's Child. She was so sweet always, one of the most beautiful people I've ever known."
—Beyonce' Knowles, (Destiny's Child),
Singer, Actress

"I Love you Aaliyah, and you're forever missed."
—Missy Elliott, Singer, Rapper

"She was the best person I ever knew.... I never met a person like her in my life. Wherever we were was like our little party in our own little world."
—Damon Dash, CEO, Roc-a-Fella Records

"She was one of those individuals that would light up a room. She always greeted you with a smile."
—P.Diddy, CEO, Bad Boy Entertainment

"Ithink I speak for all of us standing here when I say she was definitely one in a million."
—Ginuwine, Singer

"One day we will be together again."
—Janet Jackson, Singer

"*I watched Aaliyah grow up…Though she was ours for only a short time, what a time it was. I love Aaliyah and I will miss her for the rest of my life.*"
  —**Gladys Knight, Singer, Actress**

"*She was my girl; we've always been friends. It hurts.*"
  —**Lil' Kim, Rapper**

"*I think it was fly that she took chances on her music. Just the softness of how she sang over those hard-ass beats. It was something different.*"
  —**Jermaine Dupri, Producer, Rapper**

"*She could sing. She wasn't a studio singer. When you heard her live she sounded the same way she did on her album. She was about to become a mega super star.*"
  —**Eve, Rapper**

'*We were just getting to know her as this funny, engaging person, star in the truest sense of the world.*"
  —**Amy DuBois Barrett,**
    Editor-in-Chief, *Honey Magazine*

Aaliyah changed the "game" forever and left a path hard to follow. She was the Josephine Baker of our time. As a singer she inspired me to always take my lyrics to the next level. Her confidence empowered women through her music and cradled the fear of rejection for men. She will never be forgotten. Every time her fans exhale the memory of her spirit, she inhales life, forever being a part of time—embodying her music through many like my self.
  —**Khalilah, singer, songwriter, youth**
    spokesperson, The Stay Strong Foundation

Publisher's Note

I am a fan, a true fan, of Aaliyah's who has danced to, listened to, sung to and been mesmerized by the lyrics and her vocals floating through the beats—floating, soaring above the electronic music as a whisper in your ear—going deep into all of our souls.

When Kelly Kenyatta and I first discussed working on a book about Aaliyah, we began the discussions based upon a love and admiration for her—her music, her drama, her mystery, her spirituality, her essence—her love of life. This was in early 2001. By July 2001 we had finished the manuscript; her album was dropping and we anticipated the next level of her career and wanted this book to be a celebration of her life.

We all thought that sweet girl would be with us forever and that we would have her talent and her many artistic abilities forever to enjoy. Events transpired and Aaliyah is no longer with us. We shelved the book and waited for our hearts to heal. Our hearts have still not healed; and yet we play her music and remember this fun-loving, wonderful human being.

So this book remains what it was always intended to be—a celebration of a great talent and a celebration of the life of Aaliyah.

God bless Aaliyah, and God's blessings to all of you.

Tony Rose
Publisher, Busta Books

Aaliyah:

An R&B Princess in Words and Pictures

by **Kelly Kenyatta**

Busta Books

New York   Los Angeles
Phoenix

Aaliyah: An R&B Princess in Words and Pictures
By Kelly Kenyatta

Published by: BUSTA Books
A Division of Amber Books
1334 East Chandler Boulevard, Suite 5-D67 Phoenix, AZ 85048
amberbk@aol.com
www.amberbooks.com

Tony Rose, Publisher/Editorial Director   Samuel P. Peabody, Associate Publisher
Yvonne Rose, Senior Editor   The Printed Page, Interior & Cover Design

ALL RIGHTS RESERVED

Song lyrics: *Honey Love* ©1992 R. Kelly
          Bump 'n Grind ©1994 R. Kelly
          Age Ain't Nothin' But a Number ©1993 R. Kelly

ISBN 0-9702224-3-2

Library of Congress Cataloging-in Publication
Kenyatta, Kelly
   Aaliyah : an R&B princess in words and pictures / by Kelly Kenyatta.
     p. cm.
   Discography: p.
   ISBN 0-9702224-3-2
   1. Aaliyah. 2. Rhythm and blues musicians--United States--Biography. I. Title.

ML420.A04 K46 2002
782.421643'092--dc21
[B]
                                       2002018527

10 9 8 7 6 5 4 3 2 1
First Printing April 2002

Dedicated to

the families and friends of Aaliyah
and her fellow colleagues
who perished in flight
and to her millions of fans.
She lives on in our hearts.

"In the midst of working,
I know how to have fun. Enjoy your job.
You should wake up every day
and love what you do.
And I honestly do, from the bottom of my heart,
to the depth of my soul."

–Aaliyah on MTV

Contents

Aaliyah: An R&B Princess

Introduction

Aaliyah (ah-lee-ah) means "exalted one," someone of great nobility and esteem. In her 22 years
of life, Aaliyah Dana Haughton lived up to her
name. Her talent, grace, poise, and beauty ele-
vated her among the highest ranks of entertainers. Her kindness and generosity epitomized
humanity. Born into a family with show business
members, the singer-actress couldn't remember
a time when she herself was not interested in
performing. A lot of parents look at their children and wonder how they can make them
stars. In the case of Aaliyah, well, she was just
born to be a star and her parents didn't have to
push her at all. Her biography is a story of sacri-
fice and dedication, of being disappointed but
bouncing back. Aaliyah had that something
extra that super successful people have, the abil-
ity to "dust herself off and try again" because no
one knew her abilities and believed in her the
way she did. Her biography is that of a very
driven young girl who developed her skills and

made a great start for herself when she accepted the help of her family members in the business—her legendary aunt Gladys Knight, and her uncle Barry Hankerson, a music industry executive. This is the coming-of-age story of a young artist who became a major force in music and acting. It chronicles a star who, like her own favorite entertainers—Whitney Houston, Janet Jackson and Gladys Knight—was destined to become an American icon. The sun has set on this magnificent young woman, but she forever lives in the hearts of fans worldwide. Aaliyah truly is one in a million.

Chapter One
A Star is Born

Aaliyah Dana Haughton was born January 16, 1979, in Brooklyn, New York, to parents Michael and Diane Haughton. Her brother Rashad, who was two years older than she, welcomed her into their family and would cherish his younger sister forever. When Aaliyah was 5, the family moved to suburban Detroit, Michigan. The children lived charmed lives. They were good kids who reveled in each other's company. They played together and like most older brothers, Rashad was protective of his sister. She looked up to him as he exhibited creativity and an interest in movies at an early age. Aaliyah was developing a passion for show business, too. She liked dancing and singing. She danced whenever her mom put on her favorite Johnny Mathis records and she snuggled up next to Mom to watch the Oscars. Her dreamy eyes glued to the television set, the

3

young girl was in awe of the glamour and entertainment of the Oscars ceremony. When Emmy nights rolled around, it was no different. She watched the stars strut their stuff, all the hottest stars—from Michael Jackson to Madonna to En Vogue. At some level at a young age, Aaliyah started to believe she also could command an audience the way popular entertainers did. Even before she started school, she began performing. "I'd sing at the drop of a hat," she has said, looking fondly back on her early years.

While her parents did not urge her toward entertainment, they supported her. "When I told my parents that I wanted to go into entertainment, they were with me all the way," she said. "They're the ones who shuttled me back and forth to my vocal lessons."

Diane and Michael were there for their daughter when she expressed interest in acting in her first play in first grade. The production was "Annie." Aaliyah didn't get to play the leading character but she didn't mind. She was excited to have the role she got because it afforded her a speaking line. She walked onto the stage and delivered her line as though she was the star of the show. Her family beamed with pride and she was convinced right then and there that she would do a lot more acting.

When relatives and friends of the family found out what a talented ham she was, they requested her to perform at weddings. So there she would be, singing her 8- or 9-year- old heart out to songs like "Ribbon in the Sky," by Stevie Wonder, or something from Whitney Houston, like "The Greatest Love of All."

In addition to the Oscar and the Emmy ceremonies, Aaliyah found another TV show she loved and that was *"Star Search."* Hosted by Ed McMahon, the show featured some of the most promising undiscovered performers in the country. It gave Destiny's Child ("Say My Name") a chance and others who went on to be super successful including Britney Spears ("Oops I Did it Again"), Justin Timberlake of N' Sync ("Bye, Bye, Bye"), and Christina Aguilera ("Genie in a Bottle"). Aaliyah also would be introduced to the nation by *"Star Search."* She walked out onto the stage and into the national spotlight and sang "My Funny Valentine." She did a great job and the audience cheered and cheered. But the competition was fierce and Aaliyah lost, just like Destiny's Child and other acts who went on to become successful. Ed McMahon was charmed by the little girl and wished both she and her competitor could've been named winners.

McMahon said, "There's a thing you can see when somebody walks out on the stage. I call it fire. They've got that inner fire, which has nothing to do with the schooling, nothing to do with the teacher, nothing to do with the parents. There is a desire in that person to please the audience. You see enough of it to recognize it. And that's what I saw in Aaliyah."[1]

The seasoned entertainment show host couldn't have been more right. Aaliyah's primary drive came from one place: Aaliyah. "This is something I truly love in my heart. When I was 9, I'd be asking (my parents), 'Did anybody call for me to do anything?'"[2]

Aaliyah had gone from performing for her school-yard peers to performing for millions of television viewers on *"Star Search"* in 1990. Although she didn't win, she had gotten a taste of national prominence and was captivated by it. She continued to hone her vocal skills. Learning lessons in charity early on, she often performed at Detroit's Operation Get Down which was co-founded in the 1970s by her uncle. The community organization offered shelter and support to the homeless, youth development programs, GED assistance, and family emergency services.

Chapter Two
Young Aaliyah Finds a Mentor

Aaliyah's spirit was soon rejuvenated after her loss on the national television show, partially with the help of her aunt Gladys Knight (who was married to her uncle Barry Hankerson). It has been said Gladys discovered Michael Jackson and his brothers (first called the Jackson Five and then the Jacksons). She undoubtedly knew talent when she saw it and she saw it in the preteen. In return, Aaliyah deeply admired her aunt for being one of the biggest R&B stars in the business. Gladys was a beautiful, down-to-earth woman and Aaliyah knew she was blessed to have a close relationship with such a legendary entertainer. Gladys knew the ups and downs of show business so she could teach her young niece a lot. Like Aaliyah, soulful singer Gladys fell in love with performing when she was a child, too. She and her brother and their cousins formed Gladys Knight and the Pips, which today are a part of the Rock and Roll Hall of Fame. By the time Gladys was 17, the group's "Every Beat of My Heart" was one of the Top10 singles in the country in 1961. They went on to make other Top 40 singles including "Letter Full of Tears" and "Giving Up." One thing Gladys recognized in Aaliyah other than her talent, was the "fire" that Ed McMahon had seen in her. Gladys had that fire herself because she and the Pips had wanted success beyond the Top 10 and Top 40. They wanted a number one hit. It happened, but not until they made important career moves, with the first being moving to the Motown label. The company was the label of mega-stars like the Supremes, Marvin Gaye and the Temptations. Gladys Knight and the Pips recorded hits like the original version of "I Heard It Through the Grapevine," "It Should Have Been Me" and "If I Were Your Woman." Their biggest hit came in 1973 when "Neither One of Us" became the national chart's number two song.

Later at Buddah record label, the group got its first number one hit with "Midnight Train to Georgia." "I've Got to Use My Imagination," and "Best Thing That Ever Happened to Me" also became hot singles although they never reached number one. By the time Gladys took Aaliyah under her wing, the soul singer had acted in two feature films, "Twenty Bucks" and "Pipe Dreams." So in addition to giving her advice about the music world, Gladys could share her Hollywood stories as well. Aaliyah was a good student, observing Gladys and heeding her advice.

She decided she wanted to go on the road to perform in Las Vegas with her aunt but first she'd have to get her parents' permission. Michael and Diane talked it over. Their daughter was doing extremely well academically and was an all-around well adjusted, good kid. She was safe with her aunt. When they gave Aaliyah the go ahead, it would've been hard to find a happier girl anywhere in the world.

The thought of performing in glitzy Las Vegas with her aunt was dizzying. This time Aaliyah was not disappointed. She performed with Gladys for a week and the audience enjoyed her performances and gave them big rounds of applause. She fell more in love with the art.

She learned from her aunt about making music from the heart. Gladys' creed is "I don't do something if I don't believe in it." Even with the lyrics of the songs she writes, she's a stickler. "I try to paint a picture in my mind rather than think up words that rhyme," she has said.

She says she is very much aware that her music touches people's lives so she is careful what she sings. Gladys has even gone so far as saying that every song she performs has to touch her emotionally and spiritually in some way. She says she could not do a song she didn't feel good about. "Even if it was a hit, it just wouldn't be a hit for me," she said.

Aaliyah, though always fiercely independent, listened intently and observed a superstar in action. And not only did her aunt succeed as an artist, her heart was good. Gladys had been a life-long philanthropist it seems, whether discovering new talent, sharing her wealth and knowledge with friends and family or helping strangers through charitable contributions to causes like, the NAACP, battered women, child abuse, hunger prevention, and homelessness; the list goes on. Gladys' long and exhaustive list of honors include recognition by the NAACP Legal Defense Fund as a Black Woman of Achievement and the Congress of Racial Equality for Creative Achievement. She received the B'Nai B'Rith Humanitarian Award and an Honorary Doctorate Degree from Shaw University.

Aaliyah came off the road very inspired. Uncle Barry was so impressed with her maturity and capabilities that he introduced her to executives at both Warner Brothers and MCA Records. They liked her singing and told her so. But Aaliyah was very young, not even a teenager yet, the age where most record labels are not willing to take the risk. But they encouraged her to stay in school and to stay in the business because she would one day make it big. She heeded all the good advice she was getting. She continued to sing and act in local shows and productions. At the end of junior high school, she was so psyched that she applied to the Detroit High School for the Performing Arts. She sang "Ave Maria" in Italian and impressed the judges enough to be easily accepted. But that was just the beginning of a monumental year for Aaliyah. So much lay ahead for her.

Chapter Three
Aaliyah Meets R&B Hitmaker R. Kelly

B arry Hankerson was having a great deal of success in the music industry. He was managing the careers of some very talented artists and producing their albums. One of those artists was R. "Robert" Kelly, a twenty-something R&B singer from Chicago. R. Kelly and Aaliyah's paths would cross and for years it would be almost impossible for anyone to carry on a conversation about her without mentioning him.

R. Kelly and Public Announcement exploded on the music scene in 1992 with *Born Into the 90's* (produced by Barry) and soon became one of R&B's hottest new acts because the album was an instant hit. R. Kelly was a heartthrob who, standing 6-1 and buff with a smooth melodic voice, made women scream the way Marvin

Gaye and Smokey Robinson had the generation before. There were a number of bad boys and if R&B were to name one, it would have been R. Kelly. He mesmerized female audiences with his lyrics, which were sensual and seductive. He had everything going for him. He was a superb vocalist, but he was more than that. He played several instruments and wrote songs. He produced soulful melodies with a mix of funk and hip-hop beats.

Born Into the '90's was an instant R&B smash. Radio deejays constantly played "Honey Love" and "Slow Dance (Hey Mr. DJ)." On rhythm and blues stations from coast to coast, R. Kelly crooned.

> *Tonight is your night*
> *For the rest of your life*
> *So just lay back and relax and listen*
> *There's somethin' in your eyes*
> *Baby it's tellin' me you want me*
> *Baby tonight is your night*
> *See, you don't have to ask for nothin'*
> *I'll give you everything you need*
> *So girl, don't be shy, oh…just (Baby, come inside)*
> *Oh, turn down the lights*
> *'Cause there is something that I want from you right now, ooh*
> *(Give me that honey love) Give me that honey love*
> *(Give me that honey love) I gotta have your lovin', baby, oh*

Both "Honey Love" and "Slow Dance" became number one R&B hits. "Dedicated" rose up the pop charts to number 31. Kelly was enjoying his success, but his work schedule was oftentimes grueling. While his first album was heating up the chart, he and other key players at the label strategized about his next big move. The following year he released 12 Play, which would eventually sell more than 5 millions copies and establish him as one of the R&B superstars of his era. The first single, "Sex Me," went gold shortly after it was released but the record that would become synonymous with R. Kelly was "Bump n' Grind." Women went crazy when the knowing words flowed from his lips to soulful beats allowing them to conjure up the most sensual images imaginable. The radio stations turned up the airplay for him to declare there was nothing wrong with a little "bump n' grind.":

> *Sit down on the couch*
> *Take your shoes off*
> *Let me rub your body before I tear it off*
> *The honey lover man is ready to flex…*
> *…We'll start right here and work our way around*
> *I won't stop until I hear the "Ooh, ah" sound*
> *Don't front you know about the rodeo show*
> *So show me some ID before I get knee deep*
> *And tell you I don't see*

(I don't see nothin' wrong)You know I can't see nothin' wrong
With a little bump and grind, baby
(I don't see nothin' wrong)/
You know I can't see nothin' wrong
With a little bump and grind, baby.

The single rose to number one on the R&B chart and seemed to take a permanent spot. It stayed there for 12 hot weeks. The country crossed over to bump and grind the hit to the number one position on the pop chart and it stayed there for an entire month.

R. Kelly was rising at Godspeed to stardom but he didn't intend to settle at singing. He wanted to showcase his producing talents. Barry considered introducing him to Aaliyah as an artist to produce. She was quickly coming of age. She was beautiful and mature-looking for her age depending on what she wore. She could well have inspired R. Kelly's "Definition of a Hotti, or at least the title. R. Kelly, who was in his mid 20s did not admit to a physical attraction to Aaliyah when they first met, but he did admit from jump street the girl had talent. Having grown up listening to artists like Stevie Wonder and Luther Vandross, Aaliyah knew quality music so she was a huge fan of R. Kelly. She was excited when she learned she would be allowed to perform for him, but also nervous. What would she sing? Would she dance, too?

What would the self-ascribed shop-a-holic wear? Baggy pants, dark glasses, head gear, sneakers— her closets were brimming over. Aaliyah was a very reserved girl at times. Would her star quality shine through during her informal audition with the R&B star? R. Kelly, who appeared to be a confident Cassanova onstage, could also be very reserved. He might very well have been just a little nervous about meeting the brainy and attractive, well-bred young niece of his executive producer. Would she be a brat? If her performance stunk, how would he let her down without offending her? One thing for sure, he wasn't going to tarnish his newly-gained reputation as an R&B superstar by endorsing weak performers.

The day came for R. Kelly to cruise over to Detroit and meet Aaliyah. If she were shy that day, she overcame it. She decided to sing without the benefit of instruments. Her lone, sultry voice filled the air. She sensually sung the low notes, sassed her way through the middle range and forcefully delivered the upper octaves. Her innocent, dreamy eyes attentive to R. Kelly, she performed for him as though she were performing for a crowd of 50,000 in a grand arena. She fascinated him from the beginning of her song all the way to the end. When she finished, he was so impressed he could declare but one thing: Aaliyah Haughton had perfect pitch and he wanted to work with her as soon as possible.

"I knew she had something special before she even started singing," R. Kelly said. "Once she sang for me, that was just an added plus. Immediately I wanted to work with her, get to know her and become friends." [3]

As for Aaliyah, she was so happy she could have cried. Rashad was excited for her because she was happy. The two of them delighted in the moment. Her brother was always full of creative ideas so she knew she wanted his input in her recordings.

Aaliyah would spend a lot of time with R. Kelly during 1993 working on her debut album that would be released the following year. When some people heard about them working together, they asked "What's a nice girl like you doing hanging out with a sex-on-the-brain Cassanova like him?" People think he is always the same as the sexy performer they see on stage, she responded. They think of him as the guy who sings sexy music, but that's just one side the people see. She saw another side, which was "just a really sweet guy." Aaliyah maintained her family did not for a minute worry about her and R. Kelly.

The pair had tremendous chemistry in the studio. Aaliyah was still somewhat shy. When she felt like everyone was watching her, she asked that the lights be turned down. No one had a problem with a little idiosyncratic behavior as long as it brought out her best. She closed her eyes and R. Kelly fed her the lines. She sung every line with everything she had. He coached her and worked with her during long hours while they recorded songs like "Age Ain't Nothin' But a Number." It seemed the two were joined at the head when it came to creative matters. He took into consideration everything she told him and she admired his talent and appreciated the direction he gave. She put her soul into every line of every song. Like a seasoned professional, she willingly sung the songs over and over until they resulted in sheer excellence.

Age ain't nothing but a number
throwing down ain't nothing but a thang
this lovin' I have for you
it'll never change
here I am and there you are
your eyes are calling me to your hall
all you gotta do is knock and I'll let you in
then we will feel the passion that flows within
I don't mean to be bold
but I gotta let you know
I got a thing for you and I can't let go.

They laid down track after track, "Back and Forth," "I'm So into You" and "No One Knows How to Love Me Quite Like You Do." After countless lengthy sessions in the studio, Aaliyah, along with R. Kelly, with Barry Hankerson acting as executive producer, finished her 13-track debut aptly titled *Age Ain't Nothin' But a Number*. She had proven that that was certainly true when it came to working hard and producing good music. She had thrown down like the best of them. When she sung the lyrics "This lovin' I have for you, it'll never change," the object of her passion might well have been her music.

Chapter Four
Aaliyah Becomes R&B Sensation

*A*ge *Ain't Nothing But a Number* was released in 1994 and Aaliyah gained instant attention with R&B lovers throughout the country and in other parts of the world. On the national chart, her hot first single "Back and Forth" jetted ahead of R. Kelly's "Your Body's Callin'"; Madonna's "I'll Remember"; and Janet Jackson's "Any Time, Any Place (produced by Kelly)."

"I still remember how nervous I was right before 'Back & Forth' came out," the singer said. "It was my first single, and I kept wondering if people would accept it. I was surprised when it shot up the charts as quickly as it did. I was very grateful and I'm still grateful to my fans. When it went gold I had my answer, and it was just such an incredibly satisfying feeling."

The album landed in the pop chart's top 20 shortly after its release. Aaliyah was on her way. She was in her sophomore year in high school when her career took off. Walking through the corridors of the building and chatting with her friends, she reflected on what it all meant. She had made great friendships but wasn't able to cultivate them as much as she would've liked. Her career took her out of the classrooms much of the time. It was also hard on her to maintain her nearly perfect grade point average. But education was number one with her so she found time to excel in music and in school. After all, she hoped to one day go to college and then on to graduate school and receive a doctorate degree in music history. Aaliyah hired a tutor. Sure her friends missed her, but they didn't change the way they treated her. And being the unaffected person that she was, she didn't let the business affect her negatively. She stayed the same sweet, likable girl she always was. As for her family, everything was agreeable because she was doing a good job. Her parents were proud and so were her school teachers and administrators. The school had just opened in 1992 and Aaliyah was the first student to become a professional. She made everyone proud. Meanwhile, her friendship with R. Kelly was becoming closer. He was her favorite artist at the time and she was his favorite artist with whom to collaborate.

One balmy day in July of 1995, Aaliyah arrived at BET studios to tape a show with him. The two wore matching Mickey Mouse shirts and identical baseball caps, an outfit that made people around the set talk. Being a fun-loving, mild-mannered and unsuspecting girl, Aaliyah laughed and told anyone who asked that they were on their way to Disney World. The pair had important traits that made them exceptionally compatible; they were both reserved, very talented and unpretentious. They shot hoops together and Aaliyah ribbed him when she won. She talked openly and honestly about her desire to go on tour with him, to write songs with him and to sing duets.

"We are so close because we are down-to-earth," R. Kelly once said. "We don't trip. Sometimes you can get caught up in this music and it can trap you. It can change your personality if you're not careful. That's one thing my mother would always tell me, and that is what I always tell 'Liyah."

Fans wanted to know exactly how close the mentor and his "street-but-sweet" protégé were. When asked about her love-life, the teenaged Aaliyah simply said there was definitely someone special in her life but whe couldn't say who it was. R. Kelly's adoration for her was evident. "I can just look at her and write a song," he declared. "Because she is that pure."

While Aaliyah might have been that pure, young and innocent, she quickly realized she was under the adoring, yet sometimes critical and fierce gaze of the public eye. She responded like a show business veteran. Though never behaving harshly, she still refused to take a licking from the public's sharp tongue. One of the first issues she dealt with was "whether she was good or just getting by off her affiliation with R. Kelly." Her maturity, quiet confidence and humility shined through.

"I know having him on the single ("Back and Forth") helped me get attention," the soft spoken, sophisticated girl said. "Without him it would have been harder to get airplay. I'm just thankful for the break. If I had no talent and had nothing to offer, I'd probably feel funny if people were giving him all the credit. But I know I can sing and a lot of the success is because of me."[4]

The public has a way of testing its up-and-coming stars and it did just that to Aaliyah. Despite the more than 10-year age difference between her and her mentor, despite the fact that she was a minor, people speculated there was a romantic link between them. The "Age Ain't Nothin' But a Number" title to her album didn't help her case.

The rumors peaked the summer after the album was released. From night clubs to business offices to beauty shops and playgrounds, the buzz was that R. Kelly and Aaliyah got married. The reports found their way to radio stations and a few major newspapers and magazines. Some reported that a marriage license had been issued to the R&B stars. Teenage boys who adored the young singer expressed disappointment; women fans of the mid 20s sex symbol expressed shock and disbelief. But the reports were never confirmed by the singers or by their publicists.

A Jive Records Chicago branch manager said, "They're not married. You don't see no ring on her finger, right?" He attributed the story to media hype. "Robert has reached a level now where he's going to get a lot of rumors. The more successful he is, the wilder they'll get. I know Robert and Michael Jackson were talking about this. Things get crazy and they get out of hand at a certain point."[5]

Aaliyah responded by saying, "We're really cool friends. But it's a friendship, and it will continue to be a friendship." People waited to see the outcome but nothing ever came of that talk. Aaliyah later admitted that was a hard time in her life.

"It was hard for me, but my family sat me down and told me, 'You don't have any privacy. You really belong to the public, and you are under a microscope all the time.' And at (15) it was hard but it helped put things into perspective. That's just something that goes with the territory."[6]

In the future, Aaliyah's name would be linked with any number of handsome, eligible bachelors but she maintained her privacy as best she could. In some ways the experience made her stronger. She drew much of her strength and support from Rashad with whom she was still exceptionally close. "He's always been there for me," Aaliyah said of Rashad. When she had problems, she shared them with him. Being older than she, he gladly shared his wisdom with her. They discussed everything from relationships to video concepts to what to wear on stage. They even sat side by side and wrote songs together. Rashad guarded her closely and people who didn't know them wondered if he might have been her manager, perhaps a body guard or even her publicist. Being the practical joker that she was, Aaliyah told them he was her creative consultant. It started as a joke but the title stuck.

The year after releasing her album, she spent much of her time on the road nationally and internationally with Rashad traveling with her as much as he could. She was overjoyed and stunned in Japan to find kids singing every word to her songs. "Aaliyah! Aaliyah! Aaliyah," Parisians yelled out even before she went onto the stange. Touring was every bit as exciting as she thought it would be. She performed all across Europe and in Africa. People everywhere showed her love.

Chapter Five
We Are Family:

Aaliyah meets Missy Elliott, Timbaland, Ginuwine and Magoo

It was the early 1970s and a pretty 3-year-old played outdoors in the historic city of Portsmouth, Virginia. With summer breezes playing gently in her hair, the child toddled about her yard pulling trash containers together to build a stage. Visions of young Michael Jackson singing and dancing perhaps swirled in her head. As she busily moved the crates around, she noticed the carloads of people passing by. Ah, her public. Some were neighbors; some were people who lived across town. Still others were tourists beckoned by the cool blue flag that flies over the city known for its Southern hospitality. Motorists streamed in to see the 18th-century buildings, the Norfolk Naval Shipyard and magnificent ships passing throughout the city's waterways. An added treat they didn't expect was to see a girl so little standing on top of a makeshift stage singing to the top of her voice for them. The drivers would slow down or stop, then reward the talented child with applause.

Born Melissa Elliott on July 1 in Portsmouth, Missy "Misdemeanor" Elliott was a charmer right from the start. She was born years before Aaliyah Haughton, in a different part of the country, and into a different lifestyle. But the two girls had a few key commonalities that would one day bring them together in a friendship as close as that of some sisters: they had star quality; they were extremely talented and ambitious but yet unpretentious; they envisioned their success; and they had mothers who believed they could fly.

Missy's mother Pat said, "People would ride pass (our house) and they were just so thrilled to see a little girl like that singing her heart out. Everyday she'd have a new song. And when I'd walk out to the mailbox or the clothesline, I'd just let her sing." [7]

Missy "Misdemeanor" said laughing, "When I was little, I used to sit in a room…take my mother's broomsticks, line up my dolls and sing. In my mind, I pictured them screaming for me. I would go into a whole other zone." [8]

In school she focused on her music and even took up the French horn in junior high. She wrote letters to Michael and Janet Jackson. While she sat in her room with her schoolbooks open, she had visions of the Jackson siblings coming to her school and whisking her off to make her a star. But she maintains that even then, she was willing to work hard. She knew that if she ever did get a big break, she would have to be prepared. Missy formed a girl group by junior high school, wrote love songs and won local talent shows.

Often clad in Calvin Klein jeans, Missy Elliott was a fashion plate who showed a happy side at school. She became popular with classmates and was voted "class clown." She graduated in 1990 and decided not to go to college. But Manor High's class clown was nobody's fool. She became part of a girl group called Sista and pursued stardom with all the enthusiasm her straight A peers put into college.

The Sista girls got their first big break when they finagled a backstage pass at a concert and met Devante Swing of Jodeci. Missy and her fellow members went all out to make him notice and remember them. It worked. Missy persuaded Devante to let Sista audition. When he agreed, she asked friend Tim "Timbaland" Mosley from

Portsmouth to do the original music for her demo tape. Devante flew the now defunct Sista up to New York to see the full spectrum of what the girls could do. Missy laughs when she talks about the old days.

"We thought we were too hot. We tried to look just like Jodeci during that audition. We had our pants tucked in our boots. We had begged our mothers to get us these outfits. We even had our canes. We thought we were four hot Devantes," she said.[9]

Missy's meeting with Devante Swing did not result in instant stardom, but it did open some important doors for the ambitious performer. For one, she met some of the most talented hip-hot and R&B artists in the industry, including Ginuwine and Busta Rhymes. Sista also was able to land a record deal with Elektra and Missy wrote most of the songs on the album. The group released a popular single she wrote entitled "Brand-New" but sadly, the album was never released. The girls eventually split up after a string of disappointments. Meanwhile, the ultra-talented Missy kept right on pursuing what she knew best.

"I never wanted to do anything but music," she said. "I felt I had a God-given talent and I'd get my foot in the door some way."

The album deal fell through but Devante recognized creativity in Missy's writing and producing skills and circulated her name and Timbaland's in influential circles. When Timbaland came on board with Missy, he brought his cutting-edge, funky sound he calls "the Matrix," which distinguishes itself by its double-time beats, hot multi-layered grooves and creative sound effects. No doubt about it, Missy and Tim were each other's perfect complement.

People started to call for songs or ask Missy to rap on something. It would be years before she made her first album, *Supa Dupa Fly*, in 1997. Meanwhile, she was one of the hardest-working, behind-the-scenes artists writing hip-hop and R&B. She wrote hit after hit and found a natural chemistry and working relationship with producer Timbaland. In 1993, she also rapped on Jodeci's "Don't Waste Your Time." That year, she wrote "Sweaty" for Jodeci and co-wrote the group's "Want Some More."

By 1995, Timbaland and Missy were already becoming known for producing songs that distinguished themselves from the rest. Aaliyah noticed them and she really liked that about the duo. They were not copy cats. She despised people who didn't have their own style. Timbaland and Missy were fresh. When Timbaland , on rare occasion, chose to use other people's music to mix with his own, he still went with the unexpected, like the theme to a television show instead of a one-time top record. Aaliyah spent some time enjoying the fruits of her successful *Age Ain't Nothin' But a Number* album but she soon decided it was time to move ahead in her career. She teamed up with Missy and Timbaland and the three of them hit it off. Missy and Tim were working with R&B singer Ginuwine. Magoo, a rapper and Tim's childhood friend, also worked closely with them. All five would bond and form friendships that would last for years to come. They even called themselves a family with Timbaland being more or less the leader. Aaliyah, whom he quickly came to adore as a little sister, was "Baby Girl."

So Aaliyah found herself among a group of sexy eligible bachelors and, of course, public gossip was abundant. She wasn't surprised. Mostly rumors circulated about her and handsome Ginuwine but the rumors were just that, rumors. Ginuwine had known Aaliyah from working with Barry Hankerson. Ginuwine also knew the public invasion of her privacy had hurt her deeply before. Would a high-profile relationship be the best thing for her now? Probably not. Instead of dating her, he became protective of her. They were close friends.

"She went through a lot at a young age," Ginuwine said. "I made up my mind that I was not going to step to her like that. It worked out better that way, because we are friends and we can act silly. We can't be in the same room without making fun of somebody or laughing or talking about somebody. Aaliyah and I just enjoy each other's company."[10]

Good chemistry was running high all throughout the studio and they all made dynamic music together. Missy later said Aaliyah made her feel like a superstar when actually, she had not sold a single record yet. Missy was the main writer on more than a half dozen of Aaliyah's songs and Timbaland was the main producer. He crafted complicated beats and introduced intriguing sound effects, like crickets chirping on one track and giggling babies on another. Missy wrote super hits that included "If your Girl Only Knew," "4 Page Letter," "Ladies in the House," and "Hot Like Fire." Aaliyah's new album would be rich in diversity and moods because they used the contributions of a number of talented young producers. Rodney Jerkins and Jermaine Dupri weighed in, as did Kay Gee, Vincent "V.H." Herbert, Craig King, J. Dibbs and Daryl Simmons. *One in a Million* was released in 1996 and Aaliyah was especially glad to be working with her brother.

Rashad was by that time a film major at Hofstra University so he was able to skillfully and creatively put together the concept for the video for "4 Page Letter." *One in A Million* was selling twice as quickly as her first album.

Music critics even gave Aaliyah much of the credit she deserved. They praised her for her talent, poise and maturity. They compared her to the already super famous Janet Jackson for whom Aaliyah had a lot of respect. She indeed displayed a newfound artistic self-assurance.

The *Los Angeles Times* wrote: "The 17 tracks offer no shortage of great material, ranging from the teasingly witchy 'If Your Girl Only Knew' to the gently poignant '4 Page Letter.' Between the songs, Aaliyah's self-assurance and production from a variety of young sources, all of this album's winning elements are right on the money."

Aaliyah said, "From the start, I wanted the creative control and the freedom to make decisions about which direction I'd take this album. I wanted to put more of myself into the music, but at the same time I didn't want to just flip the script on everybody. First time around, I was still getting my footing. This time I just wanted to give it my all and take some chances." [11]

All facets of her life were in order. She was still maintaining excellent grades in school. Aside from that she was faced with the typical question that the average high school kids were faced with, whether to go to prom and if so with whom. Being the clotheshorse she was, she looked forward to picking the perfect outfit to wear. Unlike the average high schooler, she was performing on television, in concerts and she was traveling the world. She was having a lot of fun.

R&B and hip-hop were influencing America as much as ever and it left its mark on millionaire designer Tommy Hilfiger. Kids couldn't get enough of his red-white-and-blue fashions that were athletic with a streetwise edge. Snoop Dogg and TLC and rock stars Mick Jagger and the Rolling Stones sported his fashions. The new designer's star roster rivaled that of Gianni Versace. When he put together a national road show touring America to promote his new Tommy Jeans range, his cast included hot girls like Aaliyah and Kate Hudson. Although she had what it takes, the singer didn't aspire to becoming a model. She was just having a good time. Sunglasses were her trademark right from the beginning. She had dozens of pairs with uniquely stylish frames. She picked out fly new ones every time she traveled. She saw the Tommy affiliation as a way of having fun with fashion while promoting her music.

Aaliyah still loved performing more than anything so she was excited to be a part of live performances. She had a blast at the Budweiser Superfest in Houston the fall of 1997. She was part of an all-star line up that included Dru Hill, Ginuwine, Mary J. Blige and Bone Thugs-N-Harmony. The whole crew was into tight music and good fashions. Ginuwine took to the stage wearing a black fedora and pulling off dance moves of his music idol Michael Jackson. Mary J. Blige delivered soulful melodies and her set was especially exciting to watch. Mary J. changed clothes more than five times. Her backdrop included four lamp posts and a bridge. That night she sung a lot of hits from her latest album *Share My World*. The crowd mellowed when she soulfully delivered "I Can Love You Better," "Not Gon' Cry" and "You Are My Everything." Fans cheered her on and showed her a lot of love. Bone Thugs-N-Harmony was one of the top-selling rap groups so members set out to live up to their reputation. They went way out. They hung a huge skull at the center of the stage. Smoke and sound effects turned the atmosphere of the concert into a haunted house. Aaliyah loved anything far out and silly so she was having a great time listening to the explosions and screams. She enjoyed the music, too. The group was at its best delivering hits like "Ruggish Thuggish Bone" and "Come Into My World."

Aaliyah worked the stage during her half-hour set wearing baggy pants and a chic attitude. She sung "Back and Forth," "Hot Like Fire" and "One in a Million" and fans were on their feet throughout the show.

But she wasn't all about just having fun for herself. She was a giver with commitments to various causes including breast cancer and Alzheimer's Disease. She especially loved children and rose to the challenge of accepting the job of role model. So when she was invited to President Clinton's program "Christmas in Washington" where he thanked the Children's National Medical Center for the outstanding work they do on behalf of children, she readily accepted. She stood among a throng of famous people including Hillary and Chelsea Clinton, Glenn Close, Shirley Caesar and Hanson.

She listened attentively as the President spoke: "More than any other holiday, Christmas is for our children. We revel in their excitement. We rejoice in their growth. We re new our pledge to help them make the most of their God-given gifts. It all began with the miracle of a child, born in a manger, who grew to teach a lesson of peace that has guided us for 2,000 years now. It continues to light our journey toward a new century and a new millennium. Every child is a miracle, and it is for their futures that we must all dedicate ourselves to work for that universal, timeless vision of peace in every nation, in every community, and, most important, in every heart...May the magic of Christmas be always with you."

Aaliyah was moved by that experience. It further strengthened her resolve to give wherever she could. The more popular she became, the more kids looked up to her. She accepted that challenge as well.

"I belong to the public so I am expected to serve as a role model," said the humble, charismatic entertainer. "Everyone is looking at me and I work very hard at being a positive role model. But I am only human and I do make mistakes. I also advise that those who look to me as a role model look to their parents, too. They really should be the primary role models."

Personally, professionally and spiritually, Aaliyah was on track. She had accomplished so much, from going to prom to graduating to multi-platinum career success. Still there was more to be done. Aaliyah had another gift that needed to be shared: her acting.

Photo Gallery

Aaliyah

The Aaliyah we all knew and loved.

The sweetest girl in the world.

Aaliyah working it with one of her backup singers at the Newark Symphony Hall, 1995.

Aaliyah with boyfriend Damon Dash, CEO of Roc-A-Fella Records at Jay Z's Mother's Day dinner.

Aaliyah with Kidada (Quincy Jones' daughter), girlfriends and sisters forever. Don't they look just alike?

Aaliyah backstage at the Roseland Ballroom, NYC, with friend Shawn, her brother Rashad (foreground), and the Mighty Jay Z, 1998.

Two of the most beautiful women in the world, Stacy Dash from Clueless and Aaliyah. Aahliyah had many friends.

Aaliyah with her biggest fan and music collaborator, Missy Elliot at the Puck Building, NYC, 2000.

Aaliyah with Missy Elliot, Eminem, and Timbaland at Eminem's 2000 Marshall Mather's album release, Club One 51, NYC.

Aaliyah down with Ananda Lewis and friend at the "Back in One Piece" video shoot for the "Romeo Must Die" movie.

Aaliyah, the rising star, with Miss Jones at the 1995 Source Music Awards, Madison Square Garden, NYC

Aaliyah with K.C. and Mr. Dalvin from Jodeci, rehearsals for Source Awards, 1995

Aaliyah and R&B singer Tank, Blackground Records.

Aaliyah and her music boyfriend, Ginuwine.

Aaliyah with Missy Elliot and Jay Z

Aaliyah, Ananda, and friend having fun on the "Black in One Piece" video set.

Aaliyah, Source Awards rehearsal backstage, Madison Square Garden, 1995.

Aaliyah with Big Daddy Kane, backstage at the 2000 Hot 97 Summer Jam, Continental Airlines Arena, East Rutherford, NJ.

Aaliyah and Andy Hilfiger celebrate Tommy Hilfiger's birthday at the Penthouse 450 in New York City.

Aaliyah with boyfriend , Damon Dash, CEO *of Roc-A-Fella Records in the Hamptons at a celebrity baseball game between* Roc-A-Fella *Records and Bad Boy Entertainment.*

Aaliyah…Safe at Base!

Aaliyah

Aaliyah posing with Death Row Records Teeshirt at Source Awards, Madison Square Garden, 1995.

Baby Girl

Baby Girl

Aaliyah, the fashion queen.

Missy Elliot and Timbaland

Ginuwine

Missy Elliot

Chapter Six
A Songbird Spreads Her Wings:

Aaliyah Becomes a Movie Star

Aaliyah was enjoying a lot of success as a singer but her ambitious nature didn't let her settle at that. The acting bug bit her when she was a little girl and she was still affected. Now things looked to be working in her favor in that regard, too.

Shortly after she recorded "Journey to the Past" from the animated "*Anastasia*" in 1997, she received a call to audition for Elton John's musical "*Aida*." She auditioned and got called back twice. "I have been successful as a singer and that will always be my first love," she said. "But to have longevity in the business, you have to branch out." She was putting into practice some of the lessons taught to her by her aunt Gladys Knight years before.

She also received word the people at the Academy Awards wanted her to perform and she could hardly contain her excitement. "The Oscars is a show my mother has been watching since she was a little girl," Aaliyah said. "I have been watching it with her since I was young so to know that I'm going to be walking across that stage and singing is incredible."

This was even an occasion to wear a dress and she once said: "I tell people that unless it's absolutely necessary, you won't catch me in a dress, but this is definitely an event where I'm going to wear a gown."

Aaliyah, like other stars, could have had most any designer custom make a dress for her but she didn't. She went to a nearby mall and found a sleek, dark evening gown.

She performed in front of a world television audience alongside Michael Bolton and Trisha Yearwood. Among a crowded field of stars, her beautiful voice and stunning appearance managed to set her apart from the rest. People everywhere took notice. If they didn't know who Aaliyah Haughton was before, they were likely to remember her from then on.

The acting world seemed to be calling her name louder and more clearly. In addition to recording for the *Anastasia* soundtrack, she recorded for the *Dr. Doolittle* soundtrack. She earned a Grammy Award nomination in 1999 for its track "Are You That Somebody?" She was reading movie scripts and was handed *"Romeo Must Die"*—the story of two powerful and extremely corrupt families— one African American, one Asian—in a war to seize control over Oakland's waterfront. The two leading characters were Han Sing, a tough Chinese martial artist aiming to avenge his little brother's death, and Trish O'Day, a principled, strong-willed girl from the rival family. Amid all the rivalry, backstabbing, fighting, shoot-outs and revenge killings, and to the dismay of their families, Han and Trish find themselves falling for each other.

Aaliyah knew right away she wanted to bring the character of Trish O'Day to life. Her lucky pillow, which she nicknamed "Wilson," was getting a lot of attention from her over the years but she needed the comfort of Wilson more than ever before. Visions of herself in the role of Trish consumed her as she lay quietly on her pillow at night. She soon learned she'd gotten the role and was cast next to Jet Li. Delroy Lindo, Isaiah Washington, Russell Wong and rapper DMX were also cast. Aaliyah felt lucky to be in the line-up of talented actors. It was an opportunity for her to learn. She decided even her music would have to take a backseat to the movie if necessary. She was nervous about it all but at the same time she could hardly wait to get to the set and begin work. She found Jet Li very nice and encouraging. It was his first English-speaking role, so she helped him with his accent. Jet helped her with a fight scene, which turned out to be one of the funniest and most exciting clips from the movie. Jet's character was too much of a gentleman to lay his hands on a woman to fight her, so when he came up against a female enemy, he grabbed ahold of Aaliyah's hands and propelled and maneuvered her while she did the fierce kicking. Every single day on the set promised hard work, but gratification. Producer Joel Silver was impressed with Aaliyah's debut performance. He thought her future could be just as bright as an actor as it was as a singer. And Aaliyah had already found a way to combine the two. She recorded "Try Again" for the *Romeo Must Die* soundtrack.

She exhaled when the movie hit theatres. It received critic rankings from very good to not good. Some criticized the lack of romance between Han and Trish. Others said the script could have been better. But action flick lovers didn't seem to pay much attention to the critics. They turned out in big numbers to see the movie and made it a box office success. Fans raved about Aaliyah's performance and even the critics gave her high marks.

She also had a smash hit on her hands with "Try Again." The song racked up a Grammy nomination and she received the MTV Best Female Video Award for 2000. For that award she beat out Christina Aguilera, Britney Spears and Toni Braxton.

For its popular Movie Awards, MTV nominated Aaliyah for "Best Female Performance" and "Best Breakthrough Performance, Female" for her role in *"Romeo Must Die."* The competition was fierce. For "Best Female Performance" the other nominees were Julia Roberts for *"Erin Brockovich,"* Kate Hudson, *"Almost Famous,"* Julia Stiles, *"Save the Last Dance"* and Jennifer Lopez, *"The Cell."* The award went to Julia Roberts. For "Best Breakthrough Performance, Female" she was up against the talented Zhang Ziyi, *"Crouching Tiger, Hidden Dragon"*; Erika Christensen from *"Traffic"*; Anna Farris from *"Scary Movie"*; and Piper Perabo, from *"Coyote Ugly."* Erika Christensen won that award.

But Aaliyah was so impressive in her debut role that she was cast as a character named Zee in two other of Joel Silver's upcoming productions: *"Matrix II"* and *"Matrix III."* She soon did much of the shooting for *"Matrix II."* She also got the big role of Akasha, the 4,000-year-old Egyptian vampire in *"Queen of the Damned,"* the movie version of the book by one of her favorite writers, Anne Rice. Aaliyah jokingly commented that she would have to "tap into my evil side" to play Akasha. The vampire was the mother of all vampires, very powerful, very spoiled, very regal." This movie would likely provide her biggest acting challenge yet, but she was up for it. She boarded the plane for Australia where the crew would spend four months making the film. Again, she was impressive.

Michael Rymer, director of *"Queen of the Damned"* told *Teen People*, "Every day I'd come home from the set and say to my wife, 'That girl is amazing.' She was playing a 4,000-year-old ancient Egyptian vampire, so she had to learn an accent. She had to learn how to fly on the wire rigs. She had to wear very painful contact lenses and teeth, which she had to learn to speak with. She had a very skimpy costume, and we were out shooting all night in the freezing cold in the Melbourne winter. This girl would do take after take and never complain, never get grumpy or impatient. She was just the straightest, sweetest, most even-tempered person I've ever worked with."

Aaliyah, in all her hard work on the set of movies, had not released a CD for five years although she had contributed to a significant number of albums by other artists. Her fans were eager for her to release her own. Acting had consumed a lot of her time and she missed the studio, too. So while she was filming her movies, she collaborated on a third album when she could find time. She had become much more demanding of herself so she wouldn't be rushed into putting out an album just because she was expected to. It was in the works for a while. She worked with Timbaland and a host of new talent including Bud'da, Rapture and E. Seats, and J-Dub. Simply titled *Aaliyah*, the CD contained 14 tracks including "We Need a Resolution," featuring Timbaland, "Rock the Boat," "More Than a Woman," "Never No More," "I Care 4 U," "Extra Smooth" and "What If." It was released during the summer of 2001 from Blackground Records and made quite a splash. *Aaliyah* dealt openly with matters of the heart, for example, the hot single "We Need a Resolution" reached out to lovers who can't seem to make it work. "Never No More" dealt with the thrill of love. She tried her voice at Latin pop in "Read Between the Lines" and she performed "What If" to metal beats. "Rock The Boat" one reviewer wrote, "Is a seductive slice of soul to take your breath away."

Screamed an *Entertainment Weekly* headline. "Aaliyah lets her emotions get the best of her on her ruthlessly romantic new album." The magazine gave the album a near-perfect rating. It debuted at number 2 in the country, second only to Alicia Keys' multi-platinum *Songs in A Minor.* Other artists in the national Top 10 were D12, Staind, Foxy Brown, P. Diddy, Destiny's Child, Jagged Edge, Linkin Park and Kurupt. *Aaliyah* would go on to become yet another platinum-selling effort.

With three popular albums, 10 videos, 10 appearances in other artists' videos, a hot debut movie and contracts for more prominent films, Aaliyah had brought her career to a new level. But she knew how to enjoy her social life as well. Over the years, she spent as much time as she could with her friends. She vacationed in Fiji with her super-close friend Kidada Jones. When they couldn't be together in person, they hung out on the telephone.

Jermaine Dupri recalled in *Teen People*, "No matter how big she was and no matter what she was doing, Aaliyah never seemed like she was too busy to speak to her friends or her family or fans. Me, her, Kidada and Usher used to sit on the phone and have these long conversations. In this industry, we work so much that you don't get the chance to do that type of stuff. I remember us being able to do that. Never talking about the business, just having crazy conference calls."

Undoubtedly she talked about her relationships with her good friends because she was mum about it with the media. She was now rumored to be dating Damon Dash, CEO of Roc-a-Fella Records. She was smiling a lot. She was happy. But she was still protective of her private life. When reporters questioned her about Damon Dash, a typical answer was: we are very close friends.

She had learned a lesson early on in show business. When asked about the advantages and disadvantages of the industry, she said: "An advantage is that being in this business you get to learn a lot, experience a lot of new things and can become real successful. And the disadvantage is, of course, a good example is myself having the negative media. People may try to manipulate you and control you and those things you have to avoid. But if you maintain strong family values and you believe in God, you can be successful. So it's been tough, but I've gotten through it because I stuck with my family and my deep belief in God."

Chapter Seven
Sunset

On August 25, 2001 Aaliyah had wrapped up a three-day shoot of her video "Rock the Boat," directed by Hype Williams on Abaco Island in the Bahamas. She and the 58 crew members who accompanied her were excited having ended the shoot. The filming had gone extremely well. Much of it had taken place in Miami a few days prior and had included risky underwater scenes. A colleague recalled that Aaliyah had tried to breathe with the regulator but it hadn't worked. With William's encouragement, she finally said she would just go in and hold her breath. Everybody watching was so proud of her when she came out they cheered and Williams reportedly couldn't have been prouder. He praised her saying "That's my baby. That's my Li-li."

Makeup artist Stacey Mossop, described to *Entertainment Weekly* the atmosphere of the video shoot on August 25 on Abaco Island: "It was upbeat, a family situation, with the cast and crew gathering in Aaliyah's room between takes. Every chance, (Aaliyah) came down from taping, they were inside that room playing cards and joking around. I was sitting at the stern and there's a window that looks into her room, and she was there making monkey faces, pressing her face against the glass."

At the end of the shoot, Aaliyah waved goodbye to the crew members on the set who were not on her flight and later arrived and boarded her plane. Her mom's very close friend Keith Wallace, who was like a third parent to her, was right by her side as he so often was. Six other crew members boarded. The plane—which was later determined to be grossly overloaded and out of balance—lifted off from Marsh Harbour International Airport at 6:50 p.m. and had risen about 40 feet before it crashed into a marsh. No one survived. In addition to Keith and Aaliyah, the others who perished were Gina Smith, of New Jersey, Aaliyah's product manager at Blackground Records; Douglas Kratz, Virgin Records' director of video production; bodyguard Scott Gallin; hair stylist Eric Forman, Los Angeles; hair stylist Anthony Dodd, of Los

Angeles; makeup artist Christopher Maldonado, of New York; and pilot, Luis Morales, III.*

The news swept the world and fans mourned the tragedy. The outpouring of love was astonishing. Candlelight vigils were held in Aaliyah's honor. Web sites were erected as tributes. Thousands and thousands of grief-stricken fans posted their thoughts and goodbyes on Internet message boards. R&B stations played her music continuously. *BET* immediately produced tributes for her. AJ and Free, the hosts of *"106 & Park,"* found it hard to hold it together as they emotionally recounted their personal experiences with Aaliyah, inter-viewed her stunned friends, played her videos and talked to shaken fans in the audience. MTV also honored the artist, as did other television stations. Major magazines scurried to package features on her. In the R&B and hip-hop commu-nities, the attention that Aaliyah's passing away got rivaled that of Princess Diana of England. And Aaliyah was remembered six days later in a funeral ceremony befitting a princess.

The evening before Aaliyah's burial, fans started gathering in New York City near the Frank E. Campbell Funeral Home (which also arranged the funerals of the Notorious B.I.G., Jacqueline Ken-nedy Onassis and John Lennon). They continued to come until the crowd numbered over 1,000. "I haven't slept all night," Nima Cohran, 21, told a reporter. "I haven't really slept since it happened. I've been taping everything on the news...I want to get every piece of her." Cohran's remarks seemed to be the sentiments of the entire crowd.

After a public tribute was held, the throng of adoring fans gazed at her rose-covered casket carried in a glass-paneled carriage drawn by two cream-colored horses. The procession included her immediate family and about 100 other somber friends and relatives. Naturally Gladys Knight was there as was Aaliyah's boyfriend Damon Dash. So were Missy Elliott, Timbaland, Ginuwine, Jay-Z, Sean "P. Diddy" Combs, Lil' Kim, Mike Tyson, Mya, Usher, Joel Silver, Hype Williams, Delroy Lindo, Tank and other industry friends and dignitaries. Inside the church, the choir sang "Ave Maria." Rashad managed to gather the strength to deliver a touching eulogy for his sister. She had always been there for him, he told her mourning friends and family, and whenever he looked at the sunset, he would think of Aaliyah's smile. When the hour-long mass and funeral service was over and family members again appeared outdoors, Aaliyah's mom wept as she opened a lace-trimmed box and 22 beautiful doves were released into the air. They represented her 22 years of life.

Aaliyah Dana Haughton's most devoted fans don't think of ourselves as having lost one of the world's most promising entertainers. We simply believe that at the very moment she passed from this earth, an angel ascended into the heavens.

Aaliyah: Her Spirit Lives On

During the months following Aaliyah's death, loved ones and fans were as saddened and mystified as they were the day the artist passed away. A still-grieving uncle Barry Hankerson said many months later, "I never question God. It's just really hard to see the reason for this one." But one thing was clear, and that was that Aaliyah's spirit would be kept alive. No hip-hop, R&B or pop music ceremony was held without remembrance of her in the ensuing months. Fans hungered for her. They petitioned record labels to release her latest music and videos and for film studios to keep any scenes she had done intact.

The singer went on to win American Music Awards in two categories, Favorite R&B Album for "Aaliyah" and Favorite R&B Female Artist. She was nominated for a 2002 Grammy Award for Female R&B Vocal Performance for "Rock the Boat," while "Aaliyah" was nominated for

Best R&B Album. Talented newcomer Alicia Keys took home the honors in both categories.

Aaliyah topped the British music charts with "More Than A Woman." She received three Soul Train Music Award nominations. "Aaliyah" was nominated for the 2002 NAACP Image Award for Outstanding Album and the singer for Outstanding Female Artist. "Rock the Boat" was nominated for the NAACP Image Awards Outstanding Music Video. She won Outstanding Female Artist.

On the film front, rumors were circulating that "Queen of the Damned" might be a big box office flop and that it would go straight to the video stores. After all, who would want to see a vampire movie starring an actress who had recently died? But the big players in the studio took a gamble and decided the film would be released. The studio called on Aaliyah's brother Rashad to dub over her voice in places where a heavier voice was needed by the vampire, who was thousands of years old. As long as the production was done tastefully, Rashad and the rest of the family didn't have a problem with it. It was Aaliyah's last performance, he pointed out, and she wanted it to be a success.

When movie critics viewed the film, many of them were unkind, though negative comments were directly mostly toward other aspects of the film and not Aaliyah's performance. She had earned high marks for "Romeo Must Die" and also for "Queen of the Damned." The movie was released in more than 2,500 theaters six months after the performer died. Her fans arrived in droves on opening day to see the long awaited movie. Warner Brothers, which released the movie, noted that the audience was made up of 30 to 40 percent women under the age of 25. Certainly most of the men eagerly anticipated the lovely and talented actress's performance, even those who had only recently learned of who she was.

During the first part of the film, the audience was amused and horrified by Lestat (Stuart Townsend), who awakened in the Millennium and transformed himself into a rock star. Posthumously, Aaliyah took a bow as Akasha about an hour into the film when she was stirred by Lestat's thunderous music. Akasha radiated and commanded the screen. Beneath the full headdress, breastplate and fangs, she was clearly a powerful, beautiful and sexy being who knew exactly what she wanted and how to go about getting it. She teamed up with Lestat to rule the world, destroying everything and everyone in sight with flames. Akasha left fans gasping when she herself was engulfed by the fire but walked away in slow motion. Aaliyah wasn't onscreen as much as fans would have liked but when she was, she wowed her public as the 6,000 year-old vampire.

After the first weekend, headlines looked quite different from the scathing movie reviews that had preceded them. "Aaliyah's Queen of Damned Draws 1st Blood" and "Queen Rises to the Top Spot," newspapers announced. The movie was number one at the box office, bringing in $15.2 million in its first days. It knocked Denzel Washington's "John Q." to number two. Kevin Costner's new movie, "Dragonfly," opened in third place. Six months after Aaliyah passed away, the R&B princess reigned as Queen.

> "She was a walking creative-being so she put her soul into acting just as she did into her music. Her art was very important to her but when the cameras stopped rolling she was just another wonderful, young, enthusiastic woman."
> —*"Queen of the Damned" Co-star Stuart Townsend*

Endnotes

1   *Vibe Magazine*
2   *USA Today*
3   *YSB*
4   *Los Angeles Times*
5   *Chicago Sun-Times*
6   *USA Today*
7   *Virginian Pilot*
8   *Essence*
9   *SonicNet*
10 *New York Amsterdam News*
11 *New York Amsterdam News*

Aaliyah: An R&B Princess

Remembering Aaliyah

"Blackground is devastated with the loss of our queen. The example she showed young people will be sorely missed and we hope her short time on earth will be an inspiration to young people all over the world. We are equally distraught by the passing of our Blackground family members Gina Smith and Keith Wallace. Their hard work and dedication were an invaluable contribution to the success of Aaliyah and Blackground. Our prayers go out to all the families.
—Blackground Records

"I'm literally praying every day for her family. Because to lose a child is like losing a leg or an arm."
—Shirley Caesar, Gospel Legend

"I've never met her, but I was devastated when I heard. I think it touched home with a lot of people everywhere, being that she was so young, so talented and so beautiful. She'll always be a beautiful girl. That will never end."
—Blu Cantrell, Singer

"Life is really, really precious. I just want to send out my deepest sympathy and love to Aaliyah and her family. That's the most important thing, life and appreciating it."
    —Mariah Carey, Singer/Actress
     (who was taking an emergency sick leave
      from the business)

"She was a reliable, committed, positive and respectable talent who unselfishly gave herself to those around her. She was our pride and joy."
    —Denise Davis-Cotton, Principal,
     Detroit High School for the Performing Arts

"Aaliyah was a beautiful person, with an exhilarating spirit and a relentless passion for life and art. Her memory and her artistic contributions will forever be with us. Our prayers go out to her family, and to the family and friends of those who lost their loved ones in this tragic accident."
    —Creative Artists Agency

"She was the best person I ever knew...I never met a person like her in my life. Every day that we were together, we cherished. Every memory, every day was a special event, whether it was going to a store or going to a movie or just sitting in a house. Wherever we were was like our own little party, in our own little world."
    —Damon Dash, CEO of Rock-a-Fella Records

"She was one of those individuals that would light up a room. She always greeted you with a smile. Her time was coming; [she] was just about to explode."
—P. Diddy, CEO of Bad Boy Entertainment, Rapper, Clothing Line Owner

"Aaliyah had gone from a household name in the urban world to crossing over successfully through her music and recent film roles. We were just getting to know her as this funny, engaging person, a star in the truest sense of the word… Also, there aren't that many strong, making-it-happen females for young women to look up to, so she was a fabulous role model. She was dynamic, smart, sexy and respected herself, making it on more than just her looks alone. Early in her career, in fact, Aaliyah took pains to not be considered a sex object, hiding under baggy clothes and behind shades. It's only recently that she's revealed her sexy side, and not because she needed to."
—Amy DuBois Barnett, editor-in-chief, *Honey Magazine*

"I think it was fly that she took chances on her music. Just the softness of how she sang over them hard-ass beats, it was something different."
—Jermaine Dupri, Producer-Rapper

"I didn't write anything. I just felt like I had to come from the heart. And I love you, Aaliyah, and you're forever missed,"
> —**Missy Elliott, Singer/Writer/**
> **Music Executive at Aaliyah Tribute**
> **MTV 2001 Video Music Awards**

"She was a beautiful sista, both inside and out. Aaliyah was an exemplary role model and inspiration for young people around the world. Aaliyah raised the bar by setting a positive, new standard for women in the music industry. May she rest in eternal peace."
> —**Egypt, Television/Radio personality**

"Everytime I saw her she had the same sweet attitude. And she could sing. She wasn't a studio singer. When you heard her live, she sounded the same way she did on her album. She was about to become a mega-superstar."
> —**Eve, Rapper**

"Aaliyah was deeply loved and will be so deeply missed. I think I speak for all of us standing here when I say she was definitely one in a million,"
> —**Ginuwine, Singer at Aaliyah Tribute**
> **MTV 2001 Video Music Awards**

"Her death won't seem real for a while. It's mind-boggling to imagine someone who was so full of life, always smiling, being suddenly dead. This is definitely the end of something; and not just the life of one individual. This is a deep moment to ponder."
>   —**Stacy Gueraseva, former editor-in-chief,**
>   **One World**

Aaliyah's family is devastated at the loss of their loving daughter and sister. Their hearts go out to those families who also lost their loved ones in this tragic accident.
>   —**Haughton Family Statement**

"I am truly happy to have been given a gift like you, Aaliyah."
>   —**Rashad Haughton, the artist's brother**
>   **(aspiring filmmaker) fighting back tears**
>   **during Aaliyah Tribute—MTV 2001 Video**
>   **Music Awards**

"The world will never get to see how her gift could have developed, and that is truly a loss."
>   —**Ernie Isley, Singer**

"One day we will be together again."
>   —**Janet Jackson, Singer-Actress**

"She grew like crazy from the time I worked with her to the stuff she's doing now."
>   —**Rodney Jerkins, Music Producer**

"No one could find a bad word to say about her…She was my girl. We've always been friends. It hurts."
        —**Lil' Kim, Rapper**

"She was like one of my daughters; she was one of the sweetest girls in the world. She vacationed with me and my family together in Fiji. I loved her and respected her and I am absolutely devastated."
        —**Quincy Jones, Producer, Arranger and Composer (father of Kidada, one of Aaliyah's closest friends)**

"I watched Aaliyah grow up, and, with the rest of the world, saw her achieve success with her very special and unique talents. From an early age, I knew she had enormous talents, an intrinsic gift…She brought joy to my heart, and I felt blessed to encourage and support her professionally and personally as she strove for each new goal. Her star had just begun to shine so brightly. Though she was ours for only a short time, what a time it was. I love Aaliyah, and I will miss her for the rest of my life."
        —**Gladys Knight, Singer-Actress**

"We eventually saw it (TV news), the whole tour bus was all in tears. Aaliyah was the first person to embrace Destiny's Child. She was so sweet always, and she was one of the most beautiful people I've ever known on the inside as well as on the out. She was so sweet and talented and it's just tragic. It's very sad. Our makeup

artist was also on the plane. Every night we pray for her family and everyone else's family."
 —Beyoncé Knowles (Destiny's Child)
 Singer/Actress

"I accept this award for her. Because she was so talented, I know she would be up here someday, accepting this Lena Horne award. So here's to Aaliyah."
 —Patti LaBelle, Singer, at Soul Train Lady of
 Soul Awards

"I heard of the devastating news and am deeply saddened... She was a wonderful and talented artist who will be missed by everyone whose lives she touched."
 —Jet Li, Actor-Martial Artist

"She was young, she was talented, she knew what she wanted, and she was smart enough not to get caught up in drugs and alcohol and all that stuff that fame sometimes gives you."
 —Stephanie Lowery, Fan, Sophomore,
 Rufus King High School in Milwaukee

"I just saw Aaliyah last Monday. She was on my radio show. She was glowing almost; she seemed really happy. When something like this happens, you can't be angry. It's just sad. It's awful. But I was talking to a friend, and he said that she's going to live forever now. I liked that he said that. It made me feel better. She's going to be a legend for our generation—our Princess Diana, so graceful, so sweet and so encouraging."
 —Angie Martinez, DJ and Rapper

"I was blown away at how friendly she was (at a photo shoot). She was concerned about how I was—if I was feeling okay, if I was uncomfortable. You don't get that from many stars at her level, and I was really impressed by that. She had such a full career ahead of her...It's truly sad. What struck me about her was how down-to-earth she really was. She was just an angel of a human being."
—**Mark McGrath, Singer**

"It's a real tragedy. I think the world is better because she was around. She is definitely going to be missed. Somebody so young and so beautiful and so talented who was just about to show us how she can be a super, super, superduper star.
—**Brian McKnight, Singer**

"There's a thing that you see when somebody walks out on the stage. I call it the fire. They got that inner fire, which has nothing to do with the schooling, nothing to do with the teacher, nothing to do with the parents. There is a desire in that person to please the audience. You see enough of it to recognize it. And that's what I saw with Aaliyah."
—**Ed McMahon, "Star Search" Host**

"In hip-hop there are so many stupid people who toy with the idea of death, it's a painful awakening when real life intrudes and removes someone of genuine heart and worth."
—**Robert Morales, Journalist/Editor**

"Life. Positivity. Humor. Sex appeal. That's what we're about. That's what Aaliyah was about."
—**Barbara O'Dair, Managing Editor,** *Teen People*

"Aaliyah visited our morning show recently for an in-studio interview. Her warm and genuine spirit lit up the room. She was a talented, gorgeous, articulate, graceful and classy lady. I was horrified when I heard the news of her untimely death. I'm comforted by knowing that Aaliyah didn't suffer, and that her spirit is resting with God. My thoughts and prayers go out to her family and the families of the other passengers who also lost their lives. We will truly miss Aaliyah, our beautiful angel."
—**Russ Parr,, "Russ Parr Morning Show with Olivia Fox"**

"I had the great fortune to meet her a few times. Aaliyah was a beautiful girl, a beautiful spirit."
—**Keanu Reeves, Actor, "Matrix" Star**

"Aaliyah was a young queen."
—**Michael Rymer, Director of** *Queen of the Damned*

"She was a beautiful woman."
—**Jill Scott, Singer**

"Aaliyah reached down somewhere and found this place where she could be this incredible actress. She was a fantastic girl."
—**Joel Silver, Producer of "The Matrix"**

"I took her around to radio stations (when she was younger)—and she was very mature for her age. One of her parents was always with her. I remember meeting her father the Saturday night she played The Apollo, opening for Blackstreet. They were all so nice. Then one other time, we had just done Hot 97, and we went to McDonald's to eat. Who was there but MC Lyte, and Lyte kept telling her, 'You're dope!' Of course, Aaliyah was saying the same to her. They were so happy to meet each other. My favorite song of hers was 'Let Me Know.' I used to run that record all the time. She just sounds so beautiful, so sweet, and that's what she was."

> —Eric Skinner, former Promotion Executive at
> Jive Records

"She was like blood, and I lost blood. Me and her together had this chemistry. I kinda lost half of my creativity to her. It's hard for me to talk to the fans right now. Beyond the music, she was a brilliant person, the (most special) person I ever met."

> —Timbaland, Music Producer-Singer-Rapper-
> Screenwriter

"She was like my li'l sis, she'd come up and put her arm next to me like, 'Listen, we gonna make this song together. I don't want you to do just one verse and it's over. We gonna do the hook together."

> —Treach, Rapper

"It's just sad because she's supposed to be here…What soothes my soul is that she was able to live out her dreams and a lot of goals while she was here."
　　—**Tyrese, Singer**

"The worldwide Virgin family is devastated by the news of this terrible and tragic accident and our hearts and thoughts go out to all those families who lost loved ones. Aaliyah, one of the world's brightest and most talented stars, will be mourned by all who loved her and loved her music. Her depth and versatility as an artist was matched by the passion and devotion she had for her craft. We extend our deepest sympathies to the family of Virgin staff member Doug Kratz. "
　　—**Virgin Records**

"She made the dullest party exciting."
　　—**Usher, Singer**

"It's always a tragedy when someone so young and gifted dies unexpectedly, but it's especially sad when it's someone who meant so much to so many people. Aaliyah inspired a lot of young people to work hard and be dedicated to what they love. She was smart, worked hard and didn't give up who she was or what she believed in. She's grown and developed before our eyes, blossoming from a teen superstar who used to hide herself behind dark glasses into this beautiful woman, a multi-platinum powerhouse. It's like we got to witness as she watched her own dreams come true. Who knows

what else she would've been able to contribute to music, film...and just life overall? To see so many young people lose their lives is horrible and sad. It's another sad day for hip-hop, the urban community and the music world ... we've yet again lost one of our heroes."
— **Emil Wilbekin, Editor-in-Chief,** *Vibe*

"She was a very happy person. She had nothing but love to give to others and she selflessly shared much of who she was. I don't know if anyone really understands that about her...As a performer, she was one of the best I have ever seen do what she does...
—**Hype Williams, Video Director**

"I for one will not be sad or mourn her death, but celebrate her life and be thankful for her gift that's touched so many. We haven't lost anyone. We've only gained an angel."
—**K, 19-year-old fan from Decatur, Georgia.
Read by Janet Jackson on MTV 2001 Video
Music Awards.**

Sources: *bet.com, mtv.com, Milwaukee Journal Sentinel, Teen People, sonicnet.com, cdnow.com* and the *Seattle Times*

Scholarship/Memorial Information

Aaliyah Memorial Scholarship Fund
First Independence National Bank
44 Michigan Avenue
Detroit, MI 48226

Several scholarships will be given each year to provide opportunities for students to attend Aaliyah's alma mater.

Aaliyah Memorial Fund
c/o Entertainment Industry Foundation
Attention: Merrily Newton
11132 Ventura Boulevard, Suite 401
Studio City, CA 91604

Phone: 818-760-7722
Fax: 818-760-7898
E-Mail: mnewton@eifoundation.org

The fund will benefit the following organizations:

- Revlon/UCLA Women's Cancer Research Program Revlon/UCLA Breast Cancer Center

- Memorial Sloan Kettering Cancer Center in Harlem

- The National Breast Cancer Coalition in Washington DC

- The National Alzheimers Association in Chicago
- The Alzheimers Association of Los Angeles

Awards

- American Music Award 2002, Favorite R&B Album, *"Aaliyah"*

- American Music Award 2002, Favorite R&B Female Artist.

- NAACP Image Award 2002, Outstanding Female Artist

Miscellaneous

Black Men magazine Cover Girl December 2000 – First Place among its "Ten Sexiest Women."

Among *Teen People*'s 21 Hottest Stars Under 21 in 1999.

Aaliyah's Discography

Age Ain't Nothing But A Number 1994

- ➣ "Age Ain't Nothing But A Number"
- ➣ "Throw Your Hands Up"
- ➣ "Back And Forth"
- ➣ "Age Ain't Nothing But A Number"
- ➣ "Down With The Clique"
- ➣ "At Your Best (You Are Love)"
- ➣ "No One Knows How To Love Me Quite Like You Do"
- ➣ "I'm So Into You"
- ➣ "Street Thing"
- ➣ "Young Nation"
- ➣ "Old School"
- ➣ "I'm Down"
- ➣ "Back And Forth"

One In A Million 1996

- "Beats 4 Da Streets (Intro)"

- "Hot Like Fire"

- "One In A Million"

- "A Girl Like You"

- "If Your Girl Only Knew"

- "Choosey Lover (Old School/New School)"

- "Got To Give It Up"

- "4 Page Letter"

- "Everything's Gonna Be Alright"

- "Giving You More"

- "I Gotcha' Back"

- "Never Givin' Up"

- "Heartbroken"

- "Never Comin' Back"

- "Ladies In Da House"

- "The One I Gave My Heart To"

- "Came To Give Love"

Aaliyah 2001

- "We Need A Resolution"
- "Loose Rap"
- "Rock The Boat"
- "More Than A Woman"
- "Never No More"
- "I Care 4 U"
- "Extra Smooth"
- "Read Between the Lines"
- "U Got Nerve"
- "I Refuse"
- "It's Whatever"
- "I Can Be"
- "Those Were The Days"
- "What If"

Contributed to:
Sunset Park Soundtrack w/various artists, 1996

Young Rich & Dangerous (Kris Kross), 1996

Supa Dupa Fly (Missy Elliott), 1997

Anastasia Soundtrack (various artists), 1997

Dr. Dolittle Soundtrack (various artists), 1998

Tim's Bio-From Da Bassment (Timbaland), 1998

Next Friday Soundtrack, 1999

100 Percent Ginuwine (Ginuwine), 1999

Da Real World (Missy Elliott), 1999

Romeo Must Die Soundtrack (various artists), 2000

The Plane Crash Investigation

At press time crucial records were still lacking into the investigation of the plane crash that killed Aaliyah and the other eight people aboard. Gilbert Chacon, who co-owns Blackhawk International Airways (with his son Erik) had declined to come forward. Investigators were still seeking access to maintenance records, pilot training records and details on how the charter flight, which reportedly was not authorized, was arranged.

According to *USA Today*: The operator of the Cessna 402B charter plane, Blackhawk International Airways, had been cited four times in three years for safety violations by the Federal Aviation Administration.

Also, according to a "CBS Evening News" report, the FAA confirmed the pilot Luis Morales

III, 30, was not authorized to fly the twin-engine Cessna.

CBS and other national media, including the *Houston Chronicle* reported that, 12 days before the plane crash Morales pled no contest to possession of crack cocaine, trying to sell stolen airplane parts and two other felonies.

The *Houston Chronicle* reported: "The judge withheld adjudication on the condition that Morales successfully complete his sentence of three-years' probation. Had he failed, he would have been found guilty of the four felonies."

Federal Aviation Administration spokeswoman Kathleen Bergen said the agency was unaware of Morales' arrests. *USA Today* reported he had a spotless flight record. Pilots are required to notify the agency only of convictions.

As of press time, the investigation into the plane crash was still underway. Some of the families of passengers aboard the plane have filed wrongful death suits against the airplane charter company and against Virgin Records.

About the Author

Kelly Kenyatta is a Chicago-based writer and freelance journalist. She has written for major newspapers and magazines and holds bachelor's and masters's degrees in journalism. She is the author of *Yes, Yes, Yes: The Unauthorized Biography of Destiny's Child; You Forgot About Dre: The Unauthorized Biography of Dr. Dre and Eminem;* and *Destiny's Child: The Complete Story.*

Celebrity Photographer Walik Goshorn poses with Aaliyah

Contact Walik at 718-328-2978

ORDER FORM

BUSTA BOOKS

Fax Orders: 480-283-0991   Telephone Orders: 480-460-1660
Postal Orders: Send Checks & Money Orders to: Busta Books
Online Orders: E-mail: bustabk@aol.com
1334 E. Chandler Blvd., Suite 5-D67, Phoenix, AZ 85048

Please send _____ copy/ies of *Destiny's child: The Complete Story*

Please send _____ copy/ies of *Yes, Yes, Yes: The Unauthorized Biography of Destiny's Child* (The Original Four Members)

Please send _____ copy/ies of *You Forgot About Dre: The Unauthorized Biography of Dr. Dre & Eminem*

Name:_____

Company Name:_____

Address:_____

_____

City:_____State:____Zip:_____

Telephone: (_____) _____

E-mail:_____

For Bulk Rates Call: **480-460-1660**

Destiny's Child: The Complete Story	$12.95
Yes, Yes, Yes:The Unauthorized Biography of Destiny's Child	$ 4.95
You Forgot About Dre: The Unauthorized Biography of Dr. Dre & Eminem	$10.95

❏ Check ❏ Money Order ❏ Cashiers Check
❏ Credit Card: ❏ MC ❏ Visa ❏ Amex ❏ Discover
               CC#_____ Expiration Date:___

Payable to: **Shipping:** $3.00 per book. Allow 7 days for delivery.
  Busta Books   **Sales Tax:**   Add 7.05% to books shipped to AZ addresses.
  1334 E. Chandler Blvd.
  Suite 5-D67   **Total enclosed: $_____**
  Phoenix, AZ 85048